Luisa Rose

Die Sonnenkönigin

Ausmalbuch für Erwachsene

Bibliografische Information der Deutschen Nationalbibliothek:
Die Deutsche Nationalbibliothek verzeichnet diese Publikation in der Deutschen Nationalbibliografie; detaillierte bibliografische Daten sind im Internet über http://dnb.dnb.de abrufbar.

Herstellung und Verlag: BoD – Books on Demand, Norderstedt

ISBN: 9783743112742

When Summer on the earth was queen
She held her court in gardens green
Fair hung with tapestry of leaves,
Where threads of gold the sun enweaves
With chequered patterns on the floor
Of velvet lawns the scythe smoothes o'er:
Their waving fans the soft winds spread
Each way to cool Queen Summer's head:
The woodland dove made music soft,
And Eros touched his lute full oft.

Round Time's dial thronged the Hours;
Masking in the Masque of Flowers

Like knights and ladies fair be-dight
In silk attire, both red and white.

And as the winds about them played,
And shook the flowers or disarrayed,

A whispered word among them goes
Of how the Lily flouts the Rose,

Suitors for Summer's favour dear,
To win the crown of all the year -
And how each champion brave would fight
Queen Summer to decide the right.

Then shrill the wind-winged heralds blew;
The lists were set in Summer's view

With blazoned shields, & pennons spruce
Of fluttering flag & fleur-de-luce:

And spread with 'broidered hangings gay,
Till all was ready for the fray.

Between their banners white and red,
Of Rose and Lily overhead,
Queen Summer took her judgment seat,
Whom all the crowd of flowers did greet.

The silver arum-trumpets sound
With tongues of gold, & to the ground
The shining champions each did ride,
Their party-colours flaunting wide.

The summer winds the onset blew:
With level lance each champion flew,

And clashed together, mid a snow
Of petals on the grass below.

Pressed eager then the gazing rows:
Some cried "the Lily", some, "the Rose"
But while the fate of battle hung,
Again the silver trumpets sung;

And, sudden charging from each side,
Of Roses and of Lilies ride
A host to still maintain the strife
For roses or for lilies' life

Like a cloud of morn they bore,
Or rosy wave on grassy shore,
That, breaking, dashed the silver spray
They met – the Lily-lances play;
In crested legends on that came
Against them – snow & burning flame
Mixing with the crimson flood
Of roses & their fragrant blood,

Whereof the grass undue was rife,
As surged & rolled the Floral strife,
With checquered fortune o'er the green,
Until at last up-rose the Queen:

And caused the zephyr horns to blow
A truce, the victor's crown to show.
But like a garland on the ground
Of roses & of lilies found,
So linked & locked in strife they lay
Each silver stem & clinging spray,

The doughty champions could not rise
Before the Queen to claim her prize.
So to the field of battle down
She stepped, with rose & lily crown
Of silver & of gold fair wrought;
And thus Queen Summer spake her thought:

And to each warrior thus did say:
Read in the fortune of your fray
Fit emblem sweet of unity.
Nor Rose nor Lily plant on high,
But side by side in equal right,
And pleasant cheer the Red & White:

That men & maids be glad to see,
Alway in pleasant company,

Life & Love close linked together,
And strong to bear times wintry wea:
:ther

Love not consumed in passion's heatt
But golden flamed & stedfast, sweet:

Time's snows shall quench not, though they hide?
Each spring renews the rosy tide:

Each lover in his lady's face
Sees roses blent with lilies' grace :

The poet & the painter praise
This heraldry of summer days;

And every garden sweet that blows
Doth set the Lily by the Rose.

Peace, then in all my borders be,
Beneath the silvern olive tree. ”

Each rose, each lily's head bent low,
And each one sought his fallen foe:

And careful hands the wounded bore,
With balm and honey to restore:

And trimmed the grass & decked
each seat,
And made all fit for dancer's
feet;

Beneath the summer full-orbed moon,
Ruddy & gold that rose full soon,
Like rose & lily fused in fire,
Ere the sunset's torch expire.

Then forth each knightly lily led
A blushing rosy dame so red;

Nor lily hands or hearts denied
The rose-hued warriors erst defied.

Light-footed through the dance's maze,
Quick they moved like wingéd fays;
As measured music soft did swell,
And echoed deep from bosky dell,
Till, from the leafy forest side,
The sweet-tongued nightingale replied,
Dissolved in streams of silver sound,
Merged in the moonlight, lost & found;
Like the dancers, till in shade,
Of Summer's verdant night they fade.

Weitere Ausmalbücher von Luisa Rose:

Titel	ISBN
Alice im Wunderland	9783741297502
Blumen und Märchen	9783743102002
Der Struwwelpeter	9783743102699
Die Struwwelliese	9783743102811
Don Quixote	9783743104037
Drei kleine Schweine	9783743104099
Eine Blumenhochzeit	9783743104105
Fröhliche Reigenspiele	9783743104112
Lustige Tanzspiele	9783743104273
Reise ins antike Griechenland	9783743112568
Flucht ins antike Griechenland	9783743112599
Pariser Leben im 19.Jahrhundert	9783743112704
Die Sommerkönigin	9783743112742
Der Schneider und die Krähe	9783743112827
Die Wikinger	9783743113275
Hänsel und Gretel	9783743114265
Max und Moritz	9783743103214
Schnurrdirburr	9783743112834
Mode des 18. und 19. Jahrhunderts	9783743112971
Kostümbilder des 18. und 19. Jahrhunderts	9783743114401
Abenteuer im Bienenland	9783743117051
Griechische Helden der Antike	9783743117709
Märchen alter Zeit	9783743116559

Notizbücher von Luisa Rose:

Titel	ISBN
Drachentöter (Notizbuch)	9783743113077
Natures Wonders (Notizbuch)	9783743113817
Gedankenspiel Notizen (Notizbuch)	9783743113886
Smaragd Notizen (Notizbuch)	9783743114296
Jagd Notizen (Notizbuch)	9783743114302
Tradition (Notizbuch)	9783743114319
Antik Notizbuch (Notizbuch)	9783743114326
Veni Vidi Vici (Notizbuch)	9783743114340
Black List (Notizbuch)	9783743114371
Mystic Notes (Notizbuch)	9783743114388
Magic Notes (Notizbuch)	9783743114418
Fantasien (Notizbuch)	9783743114463
Creative Notes (Notizbuch)	9783743114487
Persönliche Notizen (Notizbuch)	9783743114494
Peter Pan (Notizbuch)	9783743114531
Rose (Notizbuch)	9783743114548
Quality Street (Notizbuch)	9783743114555
Rubin Notizen (Notizbuch)	9783743114647
Schmetterlinge (Notizbuch)	9783743114661
Ali Baba (Notizbuch)	9783743114678
The portrait of a Lady (Notizbuch)	9783743114692
Shakespeare (Notizbuch)	9783743114722
Brainstorming (Notizbuch)	9783743114739
Merlin (Notizbuch)	9783743114746
Rügen (Notizbuch)	9783743114784

Möchtest du über neue Bücher von Luisa Rose per email Informiert werden? Dann schicke eine Email mit ‚Newsletter' im Betreff an Luisa.Rose@t-online.de